FOR THE LOVE OF

Beanie Babies

Contributing Writer: Denise I. O'Neal

Editorial Consultant: Holly Stowe

PUBLICATIONS INTERNATIONAL, LTD.

Denise I. O'Neal writes the "Collecting" and "Favorite Things" columns for the Chicago *Sun-Times*, which cover a wide variety of collectibles, including Beanie Babies and dolls.

Holly Stowe is an avid Beanie Babies collector and writer. Her Beanie Babies articles have appeared in publications such as *Beanie Collector* and *Beanie Mania*, as well as on the Internet. She is also the author of *Beanie Babies Collector's Guide*.

All photography by Brian Warling/Brian Warling Photography. Photo styling by Lisa Wright.

Acknowledgments:
Special thanks to the generous collectors who loaned their Beanie Babies collections for this book: Lindsay Gehrls; Kelley Hardman; Cheryl Damato; Frank Magos; Diana Petersen and her generous customer, Judy, with Diana Petersen Collectibles at 1452 Miner Street, Des Plaines, IL 60016, 847/296-6335; Marianna and Dominic Stocco; Rachel Kagan; Leah Benjamin; and Jan Schroeder.

Contents

Beanie Beginnings

If you're reading this, chances are you've become hooked on fuzzy creatures about the size of your hand. You may even consider your addiction a guilty pleasure because you don't usually get caught up in the latest fads. The craze over Beanie Babies, however, is about as far-reaching as any you'll ever see—in the toy-collecting world or elsewhere. But how did this fascination with little bean-stuffed animals begin?

H. Ty Warner is considered the "father" of these collectible plushes. In 1962, Dakin, Inc., hired the recent college graduate to help produce their stuffed animals. After 18 years with the toy-manufacturing giant, Warner opened his own toy company in a Chicago suburb. With his line of plush toys costing $10–$20, Warner came up with a design and marketing strategy for a child-sized toy that would be similar to the larger plush line but within a child-sized budget. In January 1994, the original nine Beanie Babies—Chocolate the moose, Cubbie the bear, Flash the dolphin, Legs the frog, Patti the platypus, Pinchers the lobster, Splash the whale, Spot the dog, and Squealer the pig—were introduced to the world. Six months later, 25 new Beanies made their appearance, and the collecting frenzy was in full swing.

So how did Beanie Babies become collectible so quickly? Supply and demand, of course. To limit availability and keep the product flow somewhat regulated, Ty, Inc., chose to distribute Beanie Babies through a network of specialty stores rather than larger chains. To create demand, the company worked out a schedule of "planned obsolescence" whereby certain Beanies would be retired and new ones issued throughout the year. In fact, of the original nine Beanie Babies, only Chocolate the moose is still current; of the 25 that followed, only Daisy the cow and Blackie the bear are not yet retired (as of this writing). You'll find these old friends, and all the other Beanies, displayed and described in these pages with the same love and attention you give the Beanie Babies in your collection.

As a Beanie collector or simply a fan, you may have wondered: How many different versions of Mystic the unicorn exist? Or: Why was Doodle the rooster renamed Strut? The answers to these and other intriguing Beanie questions are here. In addition, the book's themed chapters showcase all your favorite Beanies in their "natural" habitats, providing creative collectors some ideas for displaying their little plush friends at home.

As with most things, the frenzy over these little stuffed toys didn't happen overnight. Nor was the entire country taken by storm. But after two years of building strength in the Chicago area, the Beanie Babies storm developed into a full-blown tornado, with gusts reaching out to most areas of the country.

These plush toys are now sought-after by people of all ages and from all walks of life. Some buy them to make money on the secondary market, while some snap them up simply for the love of these little "babies." Whatever *your* reason for collecting, rest assured, you are not alone. And the phenomenon known as Beanie Babies may well be a part of your life for years to come.

Original nine Beanie Babies

Garden Variety

Flowers aren't the only thing blooming in this garden. These colorful Beanie Babies take time to smell the roses in this bright, sunshiny scene. Bumble the bee and Flutter the butterfly float with the clouds through the spring air, while Spinner the spider busily spins a web among the flowers. The bunny trio of (clockwise from top) Hippity, Floppity, and Hoppity blooms out of a flowerpot, while Inch the inchworm, Ears the rabbit, and Lucky the ladybug frolic in the soil.

BUMBLE THE BEE

This little bee left collectors abuzz when they learned that newer editions of the black-and-yellow Beanie would prove to be more collectible than editions with older tags. It seems that Bumble was the only Beanie from the June 15, 1996, retirement to have fourth-generation hang tags and a poem, making later issues more collectible than those released earlier. **RETIRED.**

EARS THE BROWN RABBIT

It's easy to see where this silly wabbit got his name. Ears is a velvety, dark brown hare with huge, soft ears lined in white, a white puff tail, and a pink nose and whiskers. The oldest of the bunnies in Ty's line, Ears, lying flopped down on his belly, looks like he's eaten one too many carrots. This cabbage-patch dweller said "so long" on May 1, 1998. **RETIRED.**

FLOPPITY THE LILAC BUNNY

This pastel-colored rabbit hopped onto the scene with pals Hippity and Hoppity. Hard to find during the year, the colorful trio was especially popular around Easter. However, the resurrection was short-lived. Ty retired the three floppy-eared carrot lovers on May 1, 1998. Look for errors on Floppity's tag where "original" and "surface" were misspelled. **RETIRED.**

HIPPITY THE MINT BUNNY

As difficult to find as his pal Hoppity, this mint-colored hare left collectors green with envy of those lucky enough to snare one. Now retired (Hippity joined fellow bunnies Floppity and Hoppity in the big May 1998 roundup), this little rabbit is expected to leap to new heights on most collectors' wish lists. **RETIRED.**

FLUTTER THE BUTTERFLY

Flutter emerged from her cocoon in a burst of radiant color and immediately took flight. The butterfly with black body and tie-dyed wings only lasted one year on the Beanie market, despite the fact that kids loved her brightly colored wings. As Beanie fever spread to adult collectors, this colorful creature became the Beanie to net, making her quite a rare specimen. **RETIRED.**

INCH THE INCHWORM

Inch by inch, this colorful creature has wormed his way into Beanie collections. Originally released with black felt antennae, the multicolored Inch underwent a slight change when his felt was replaced with yarn. Inch was retired in May 1998, but he was also part of the second batch of McDonald's Teenie Beanies introduced later that same month. **RETIRED.**

SPINNER THE SPIDER

Spinner, a definite contender for most frightening Beanie, spun into Ty's web of bean-stuffed plushes in time for Halloween 1997. This Beanie sports the same blood-red eyes found on Radar the bat. With a black head and legs and a tiger-striped back, this leggy spider is sure to scare up great interest.

WEB THE SPIDER

If you can stomach this itsy-bitsy spider, you'll see that she's really harmless. Web crawled into Beaniedom early and was soon replaced with the more sinister-looking Spinner. If you think this Web is nothing more than a black widow, check out her bright red stomach: She's really one red-hot mama! **RETIRED.**

SLITHER THE SNAKE

This reptile slid his way into the record books as the longest Beanie Baby created. He's an amazing 23 inches long! Slither's upper body is the same brownish green as Speedy the turtle and Ally the alligator, and his underbelly is a bright yellow. His red-pronged tongue makes him appear ready to strike. Not to fear, this snake is only deadly to the pocketbooks of those hoping to add him to their collection. **RETIRED.**

HOPPITY THE ROSE BUNNY

The last bunny in the pastel trio, this dainty little rabbit has been in great demand. Supplies of the blush-colored bunny withered away in a hurry as collectors sought to add this Easter treat to their basket of Beanies. Cute and cuddly, this bunny headed down the same trail as her friends Floppity and Hippity when Ty retired her on May 1, 1998. Look for the fifth-generation tag with a sticker correcting the spelling of "surface"; it's a "hare" more collectible.

RETIRED.

LUCKY THE LADYBUG

This lady in red has found herself in a couple of tight spots. The tiny bug, who fits snugly in the palm of your hand, evolved from a shell with seven felt spots glued on her back to a red fabric with 21 spots printed in the material. This was apparently too many spots for her small shell, and Ty changed the pattern after a few months; the more recent Luckys can be found with just 11 spots. This colorful lady was retired on May 1, 1998.

RETIRED.

Bear Necessities

These Beanie bears create quite a colorful family portrait. Cubbie, Peking, and Blackie (front, left to right) can't lay down on this job. Old-faced Teddy in teal, Peace, and violet new-faced Teddy come next. Princess, cranberry new-faced Teddy, Valentino, and Erin sit politely in front of Britannia, Garcia, jade old-faced Teddy, brown new-faced Teddy, and magenta old-faced Teddy. Behind them, magenta new-faced Teddy, Curly, violet old-faced Teddy, and jade new-faced Teddy smile, while teal new-faced Teddy, cranberry old-faced Teddy, and 1997 Holiday Teddy bring up the rear.

BLACKIE THE BEAR

This burly bear, sprawled on his tummy, looks more like a rug than a teddy. The black bear with a brown nose is one of the lay down–style bears in the Beanie line; he feels right at home with his friend Cubbie. If you look carefully at his tag, you'll see that someone must have been lying down on the job when this guy was shipped. Upon his release in January 1998, Blackie's fifth-generation swing tag had the word "original" spelled "origiinal" on the front, and the "r" was omitted from the word "surface" on its flip side.

CUBBIE THE BEAR

Cubbie, one of the original nine Beanie Babies, is actually the same bear as Ty's bean-stuffed plush, Brownie. Renamed Cubbie when he was introduced in 1994 as part of the Beanie line, this brown, lay down–style bear can cause collectors some confusion. The important fact to remember is that Cubbie and Brownie can only be differentiated by the name on their hang tags. This leader of the pack was also the first Beanie used in a sports promotion. On May 18, 1997, Cubbie was given away to children at a Chicago Cubs baseball game. **RETIRED.**

CURLY THE BEAR

Curly's napped fur makes him different from the other bears in Ty's den. A new-faced teddy, this little brown bear left collectors a bit "surly" when they discovered that there were several errors associated with him. Look for his fifth-generation tag to have the words "surely" and "original" misspelled. He also shares a style number with the cranberry-colored old- and new-faced bears.

ERIN THE BEAR

Erin, a bright green bear with a white shamrock embroidered on her chest, is one of the new-faced bears. Introduced in late January 1997, this Beanie was the second bear to be released in an announcement separate from the regular releases (Princess was the first). Although she sold for a premium price shortly after her release, buyers shouldn't need the luck of the Irish to get their hands on this one. The word is that Erin should be a lot easier to come by as time passes.

GARCIA THE BEAR

Named for Jerry Garcia, this popular teddy shares a birthday with the singer as well. Also like the late leader of the Grateful Dead, this fellow sports the tie-dyed look. Although meant as a tribute to the singer, Ty's bear landed the company in hot water with the singing Garcia's estate, earning the Beanie an early retirement. Garcia the bear has the same style number as the teal-colored Teddys in the line. **RETIRED.**

1997 HOLIDAY TEDDY

On October 1, 1997, Ty introduced the 1997 Holiday Teddy. All bundled up in a red scarf with white fringe and a Santa-style hat, the caramel-colored bear with black button eyes made a honey of an addition to collections of those lucky enough to find him. However, with the end of the Yuletide came the end of this new-faced Teddy's edition. The bear was retired on December 31, 1997. A hint to the savvy shopper: Rumors abound that he might be the first in a series. **RETIRED.**

PEACE THE BEAR

Those in the know didn't have to be encouraged to give Peace a chance. This tie-dyed Beanie flew off the shelf as if on a dove's wings, and it has proved to be one of the most difficult Beanies for collectors to get their hands on. Still current, the new-faced bear with multicolored peace symbol embroidered on its chest is very similar to Garcia. Peace can be found wearing a brightly colored tie-dyed coat or one with more muted tones.

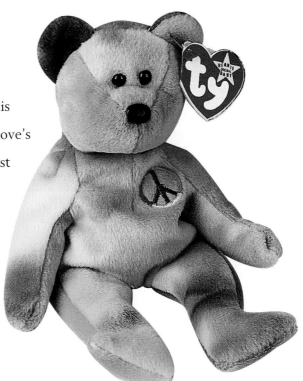

PEKING THE PANDA

Pandemonium ensued when collectors tried to get their hands on this particular Beanie. Retired before Beanie mania set in, most Pekings are well-worn from play. The lay down–style bear, who makes a great companion for Chilly the polar bear, is one of the hardest to find in mint condition. A cautionary note: Counterfeit Pekings have emerged on the secondary market. **RETIRED.**

PRINCESS THE BEAR

Like Britain's English Rose, this little bear has been well-received worldwide. Created in the memory of Diana, Princess of Wales, this royal-purple Beanie has flowered into one of the most popular Beanie Babies of all time. Released by herself in late October 1997, Princess flew off the shelf before most people were even aware that she existed.

The bear's price soon rivaled that of the crown jewels. Although listed as a current edition, there are few sightings of this bear. A note of sentiment: Ty, along with many retailers, donated profits from the sale of this rare bear to the Diana, Princess of Wales, Memorial Fund.

TEDDY THE OLD-FACED BEAR

This old bear sure has aged gracefully. The original design of Teddy, released in 1994, was available for less than one year before being replaced with a whole new look! The old-faced Teddy's posture seems to be a bit more relaxed than the new-faced version's. He also has a pointier nose and eyes set farther apart than those on the newer bears. He was released in hues of cranberry, jade, magenta, teal, violet, and brown. Talk about multiple personalities! **RETIRED.**

TEDDY THE NEW-FACED BEAR

After a little more than six months on the market, Teddy underwent quite a facelift. The resulting new-faced bears were only produced for one year, making them almost as rare as their old-faced friends. The new Teddy has a rounded face with eyes set close together, and he sits proudly among any Beanie collection. He was released in the same six colors as the old-faced Teddy, but this new version sports a satin bow about his neck. **RETIRED.**

VALENTINO THE BEAR

This white plush bear wears his heart on his sleeve. Well, almost. The appliquéd heart is actually embroidered on the bear's chest. A Valentine's Day favorite, this new-faced bear won't leave you with a broken heart. He was also given away at the New York Yankees baseball game in which David Wells pitched a perfect game against the Minnesota Twins. As a memento of the historic game, Valentino has found a new home at the Baseball Hall of Fame—and in the hearts of baseball fans everywhere.

Life in the Sea

What a wet and wild bunch! These Beanie Babies make waves in their underwater playground. Sting the stingray, Inky the octopus, Claude the crab, and Pinchers the lobster creep along the sandy ocean floor, while Bubbles, Coral, and Goldie the fish (top to bottom) glide through the watery world. Crunch the shark keeps a watchful eye on the aquatic action, and (from left) Waves the whale, Seaweed the otter, Manny the manatee, and Echo the dolphin romp playfully near the surface.

BUBBLES THE FISH

Those schooled on the fish trio in the Beanie line will know that this little lady had collectors swimming into troubled waters when a counterfeit version hit the market. The real Bubbles, a gold-and-black fish with black button eyes, appears to be cut from the same cloth as fellow Beanie, Bumble the bee. The impostor sea-dweller, although the same color, may bear a Grunt tush tag. **RETIRED.**

CORAL THE FISH

This multicolored fish is a little green around the gills. Another of the tie-dyed Beanies, Coral's color can feature shades of orange, green, blue, yellow, and brown. This tropical beauty was the first in the fish trio to be retired. And, like the other tie-dyed plushes, she is quite desirable. Coral is also suspected of having a low survival rate, putting collectors who own her right in the swim of things. **RETIRED.**

CLAUDE THE CRAB

This tie-dyed Beanie from down under—the sea, that is—was introduced at the same time his predecessor, Digger the crab, was retired. Although Claude's colors (earth-tone tan, brown, and rust mixed with splashes of blue and purple) are more muted in tone than other tie-dyed Beanies, this sea creature still makes for a bright addition to any collection. If his claws don't grab you, his color will!

CRUNCH THE SHARK

This jagged-toothed guy had collectors heading for retailers as soon as he hit the water...uh...market. More popular with boys, Crunch, the bluish gray shark with jaws flexed to bite, was another Beanie to cause a copyright stir—he shares a name with both a breakfast cereal and a chocolate bar. Although only released in January 1997, Crunch is prominent on the Top 10 list of Beanies that collectors predict will be retired soon!

DIGGER THE CRAB

Collectors saw red when Ty changed the color of this marine-life Beanie. Released with the second batch of Beanie Babies, Digger was originally produced in orange. But, possibly because people naturally picture crabs as bright red, Digger's color was changed about a year after he hit the market. If you're looking to get your claws on the original Digger, expect to shell out a tidy sum. **RETIRED.**

ECHO THE DOLPHIN

Am I blue? Echo the blue dolphin certainly was when she floundered off the assembly line wearing the wrong tag. A mixup occurred between her and Waves the whale, leaving the dolphin mistakenly labeled. Although an entertaining mammal, this seaworthy Beanie was not named for the video game with the same name. On May 1, 1998, this Beanie was cast ashore, ending all rumors of an impending trademark-infringement problem. **RETIRED.**

FLASH THE DOLPHIN

This playful gray dolphin had a few tricks in store for collectors. Issued as a member of the original nine Beanie Babies, Flash has often been confused with the later-issued Manny the manatee. Further confusing is the fact that Flash and Manny were retired on the same day. Those who think they have Flash lurking about in their pool of Beanies should look for a white underbelly and fin on her back. **RETIRED.**

GOLDIE THE GOLDFISH

Goldie swam into Beaniedom ahead of the other fish in Ty's trio. Her bright orange plush makes it easy to see where Goldie gets her name. Whether alone or with deep-sea buddies Bubbles and Coral, this little fishy makes a great addition to the Beanie collection. She's certainly been reeling in collectors ever since her retirement. Goldie was also one of the original Teenie Beanies offered by McDonald's. **RETIRED.**

INKY THE OCTOPUS

This leggy sea creature's reincarnations have almost outnumbered his legs! Originally introduced in a shade of taupe, Inky first appeared without a mouth. The octopus was all smiles when Ty gave him a mouth shortly after his release. Still not satisfied with the eight-legged critter, Ty began to think pink and changed Inky's color. Inky was justly retired on May 1, 1998. **RETIRED.**

MANNY THE MANATEE

Ty's beached manatee found life at sea a bit rough. Tossed into the pool of Beanies, Manny barely managed to stay afloat. Collectors often had her confused with Flash the dolphin due to their similar appearance. A closer look at the gray sea cow reveals that Manny has a flatter, broader body and head, and black threading on her snout. She's also a solid gray, while Flash has a white underbelly. An interesting fact: Manny's price has increased more than Flash's in retirement. **RETIRED.**

STING THE STINGRAY

Ty's cool-blue Beanie easily sailed into collectible waters. But unraveling tales about this Beanie can lead collectors to distraction. Some Stings have been seen with their tails coming apart at the seams. Barring those isolated incidents, the beautiful sea blue-and-green tie-dyed plush is as graceful as his real-life counterpart. You won't find him swimming in the ocean, however. This enchanting sea creature can be found swimming among the smart buyer's sea of Beanie Babies. **RETIRED.**

SPLASH THE WHALE

This Beanie certainly made a big splash when he was introduced as part of the original nine Beanie Babies. Splash, the jet-black whale with white belly, swam into captivity still reasonably priced. But these days, collectors who hope to net this seafaring Beanie better expect to pay a whale of a price for him! **RETIRED.**

SEAWEED THE OTTER

Ty's brown plush critter is "otterly" appealing. This bean-stuffed water dweller can be found reclining on a bank next to the water's edge. Stretched lazily on her back, she nibbles on a piece of—what else—seaweed! A playful addition to any collection, this little Beanie is an important part of any healthy Beanie collector's diet. Many collectors expect Seaweed to soon join her partner Seamore the seal in retirement.

WAVES THE WHALE

This whale set the sea rocking when he replaced Splash in Ty's saltwater world. He and Echo the dolphin were released wearing one another's hang tags. Just like his predecessor, Waves is black with a white belly. This Beanie Baby did swimmingly until Ty retired him with the now-famous group of 28 on May 1, 1998. **RETIRED.**

PINCHERS THE LOBSTER

This red lobster clawed his way through Beaniedom for quite some time. Pinchers, one of the original nine Beanie Babies, was finally retired on May 1, 1998. He also earned a spot among the second collection of McDonald's Teenie Beanies. The pinch is now on for those who haven't added this one to their Beanie roster. A hint for collectors: Some lobsters have hang tags with the name "Punchers" on them, even though the name was officially changed to Pinchers before the original nine Beanies were released. **RETIRED.**

Forest Friends

Surrounded by majestic mountain peaks and pristine water, this busy forest clearing almost echoes with the sounds of nature calling. Hoot the owl and Baldy the eagle trade birdcalls from amongst the trees as they get a bird's-eye view of the action below, while Radar (left) and Batty the bats hang out between them. Ringo the raccoon explores the riverbank as Bucky the beaver takes a refreshing dip; Stinky the skunk, Sly the fox, Nuts the squirrel, and Chocolate the moose play on the leaf-covered ground.

BALDY THE EAGLE

What an ego! We mean eagle. This proud bird not only represents a national treasure, he's also the first of the professional-basketball Beanies. In January 1998, Baldy was used as a premium at a home game for the NBA-franchise Philadelphia 76ers. Given the city's historic significance, the white-domed bird with black body and bright gold beak was the perfect giveaway. Baldy was part of the largest Ty retirement to date when 28 of the bean-stuffed plushes bid a fond farewell on May 1, 1998. **RETIRED.**

BATTY THE BAT

Now here's a novelty: a Beanie that actually hangs around...literally! Batty, the pinkish brown bat with Velcro hook-and-loop fasteners on his wing tips, is perfect for little hands that tend to lose things. Hanging from a wrist or stuck on your clothing, this furry little critter will really grow on you. The second bat in the Beanie line, this cute little night creature is the perfect companion to be "stuck" with all day.

BUCKY THE BEAVER

If you're looking to cut your teeth in the collecting game, picking up Bucky would be a good start. The brown plush beaver with black paddle-style tail proved to be slightly less popular than other Beanies. And while the bucktoothed Beanie may not be so attractive, his price is. Those interested in collecting retired Beanies should pick up the waterlogged Bucky while he's still available at an affordable price. **RETIRED.**

STINKY THE SKUNK

This little stinker caused collectors' heads to turn, but not from his awful scent! Similar in body style to Sly, Bucky, and Ringo, this Beanie earned his stripes by distinguishing himself from the others with a wide band of white down his back and tail. Unlike a real skunk, notorious for emitting noxious fumes, Ty's bean-stuffed version won't smell up your collection—unless it's from the sweet smell of success.

HOOT THE OWL

What a hoot! This night owl's fourth-generation tag had the word "quite" misspelled "qutie" in its poem. At only six inches tall, this brown-and-blush bird with big black eyes is also one of the smallest Beanie Babies. Wise collectors should have added this Beanie to their collections before Ty retired him in October 1997. **RETIRED.**

NUTS THE SQUIRREL

This squirrelly Beanie with his big, bushy tail had collectors going nuts trying to gather him up! The brown-and-white squirrel with the soft, fluffy tail has been very popular with collectors of all ages. Perched on his hind legs, this bag of beans appears to be begging for a nut or two before scrambling up the nearest tree. You might want to pick up one of these skittish little guys while he's still available and "squirrel" him away for the future.

RADAR THE BAT

This bat is one scary dude. Radar, the black bat with blood-red eyes, might be perfect for Halloween, but nestled among the other Beanie Babies he's a bit of a fright. Wings spread and eyes glaring, this night creature was ready to bite into the vein of Beanie mania. The fact that his sinister look is so different from the other stuffed animals in Ty's zoo of Beanies might help his value. The smart collector's radar probably zeroed in on that fact, making Radar a popular buy. RETIRED.

RINGO THE RACCOON

This Ringo, although not a "star" among Beanies, is still a class act. Ty's raccoon is very similar in shape to Sly the fox, Stinky the skunk, and Bucky the beaver. But his unique qualities may be hidden behind his mask—a feature that helps him stand out in the crowd. Still current, this Beanie Baby can be found at an affordable price.

SLY THE FOX

This clever little fox had a bellyful of trouble when he was first released. Originally produced with a brown belly, Sly was soon reissued with a more physiologically correct white belly. While the value of Sly is still a tricky matter, it's estimated that the brown-bellied Sly will become the one with the more valuable pelt. Don't expect to be a skinflint when this one is retired.

CHOCOLATE THE MOOSE

This chocolate moose has been a sweet treat for the entire family. Kids love the brown animal with his bright orange antlers, while adults appreciate the clever play on words used for his name. One of the original nine Beanies, Chocolate will receive his just desserts when he is retired—whenever that may be. Chocolate was also issued as a Teenie Beanie in the first McDonald's promotional giveaway.

The Kennel Club

Pound puppies and purebreds, these pooches create quite a scene as they gather on the street corner. Weenie the dachshund howls at the moon while Scottie the Scottish terrier and Tuffy the terrier hurry to join in the fun of Bruno, Dotty the Dalmatian, and Wrinkles the bulldog, who are sniffing around last night's garbage. Pugsly the pug, Doby the Doberman, and Spunky the cocker spaniel (left to right) are all boxed up, and it looks like Rover has a bone to pick with the rest of the pups. Bernie the St. Bernard watches over the pack from his perch behind the fence as Bones peers out from underneath.

BERNIE THE ST. BERNARD

When it comes to finding a purebred among Ty's pack of Beanie dogs, it's Bernie to the rescue. This lovable, four-legged beast makes it easy to see why dog is human's best friend. The brown-and-white canine with floppy black ears was among the second release of Beanie purebreds— dogs who carry their breed as part of their name. Big, sad eyes and an upturned face make it hard for collectors to resist this bean-stuffed pup.

SPUNKY THE COCKER SPANIEL

This frisky little fellow is full of spunk. The blond-colored spaniel with floppy, curly-haired ears bounded into the market full of energy and ready to go. And go he did! As soon as stores could stock the bean-stuffed pup, he flew off the shelf. That's no surprise considering Spunky is as cute as the real dog after which he's modeled. Like the other Beanie dogs, this one is ever popular.

BRUNO THE DOG

This feisty little character's bark is far worse than his bite. When the little brown pup was first whelped, his pictures made him out to be quite a brute. Not dissuaded by his scowl, collectors quickly fell in love with the cantankerous mutt. Although not a member of Ty's purebred litter, Bruno is just as popular as the carefully bred bunch. Those interested in his pedigree believe he's a bull terrier.

DOTTY THE DALMATIAN

It might be hard for Beanie lovers to spot the difference between Dotty and her pal Sparky. Both Dalmatians share the same style number, and Dotty has been found wearing Sparky's hang tag on occasion. Connecting the dots on that puzzle is a challenge for most collectors! Just remember, Dotty has a black tail and ears; Sparky's are white.

DOBY THE DOBERMAN

Before this black-and-rust pup cut his teeth as one of the Teenie Beanies in the second McDonald's promotional blitz, he was already one of the favorites in Ty's popular dog line. A member of the purebreds, Doby the Doberman is one you will not want to miss out on owning. Smart collectors shouldn't "paws" when adding this one to their collection.

PUGSLY THE PUG DOG

This Ty puppy appears masked, but he can't hide his lovable mug. Pugsly, a cream-colored dog with black pug snout covering half his face, is an adorable addition to any collection. The wrinkled pup with pointed ears and curly tail is still current; there should be plenty of these chubby little pups to create quite the cute pack of pooches.

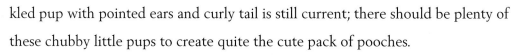

ROVER THE DOG

The release of this Beanie wasn't child's play when it came to licensing. Some might consider him a knock-off of Norman Bridwell's Clifford, the big red dog from the children's book and television series. The lolloping pooch also shares the name of a popular childhood game. Remember "Red rover, red rover, send [someone] right over"? In either case, Rover survived until Ty's May 1, 1998, retirement announcement. **RETIRED.**

SCOTTIE THE SCOTTISH TERRIER

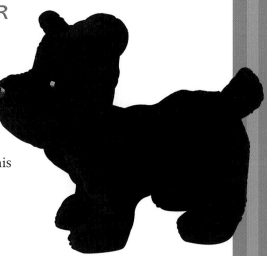

Great Scott! This Beanie Baby has two birthdays! Some of the dogs also have tags with the word "always" spelled as "slways." An all-black terrier with napped fur, this petite Beanie with stubby legs can be found running with Ty's pack of purebreds. Add this one to your collection of bean-stuffed barkers if you can. Scottie was retired on May 1, 1998. **RETIRED.**

SPARKY THE DALMATIAN

Sparks flew when Ty's Dalmatian came into play. A trademark dispute with the National Fire Protection Association ensued with this offering. Only a few of these pups were rationed from Ty's kennel before the fire engine–chasing pup was replaced with Dotty. Almost identical, the two dogs can be differentiated by their ears and tail: Sparky's are white with spots; Dotty's are solid black. **RETIRED.**

SPOT THE DOG

Ty's production line left this dog spotless. After being introduced as one of the original nine Beanie Babies in a white plush with black ears and tail, Spot later appeared with a black patch on his back. Whether to live up to his name or just to give him a trademark feature, the change was made. But the smart collector knows the Spot without his spot is much harder to find than the newer edition. **RETIRED.**

TUFFY THE TERRIER

This tough little brute lives up to his name. Tuffy the brown-and-black terrier looks ready to take a nip or two at collectors' hands, but it's more likely he'll be taking a nip out of their pocketbooks instead. You certainly won't find this frisky canine cutting his teeth on a bone; popularity is more to his liking. Look for earlier editions whose tags have Tuffy's name spelled in all capital letters.

WEENIE THE DACHSHUND

This little wiener is one hot dog! With short legs and a long, narrow body, Ty's light brown pup might not win a beauty contest. But his bug eyes and loads of character make Weenie a blue-ribbon winner among the Beanie dogs. You won't be barking up the wrong tree if you add this Beanie to your collection, especially since Ty retired Weenie on May 1, 1998. **RETIRED.**

BONES THE DOG

This homely mutt is no bag of bones. The caramel-colored dog with floppy brown ears and a pointer tail seems to have a bit of a paunch as he stretches out on all fours. He also appears to have a trace of bloodhound in his family tree. With black button eyes and a shiny black nose, this laid-back pup looks like he could sniff out the clues in a mystery. Bones was retired May 1, 1998. He was also one of the 12 Teenie Beanies in the second McDonald's giveaway. **RETIRED.**

WRINKLES THE BULLDOG

Another popular pooch in the bunch, this adorable little guy with the scrunched-up face just begs for a scratch behind the ears. Try catching this one and you'll need more than a leash to keep him from bounding away. The tan-and-white Beanie, like all the other Ty dogs, is a necessity for bullish collectors. Who could resist his wrinkled little mug?

On Safari

Roary the lion may be king, but he's not the only Beanie in this jungle. Kiwi the toucan soars over the plains, perhaps frightened by Blizzard the tiger who lurks in the trees. Bongo the monkey swings by his tail from jungle branches; Congo the gorilla munches bananas on the ground nearby as Twigs the giraffe searches for leaves for lunch. Peanut the elephant sprays Happy the hippo while Happy bathes in the watering hole, and Stripes the tiger, Spike the rhinoceros, and Ziggy the zebra gather in the brush. Freckles the leopard hunts for prey in the foreground.

BLIZZARD THE TIGER

Amidst rumors of retirement at the onset of her release, Blizzard, the black-and-white tiger, had collectors wondering if this cat would be as elusive to snare as the snow-mountain predator for which she was named. More rumors emerged after a forged picture of the cat's tag bearing the name "Snowball" was circulated. The rumors soon ran their course, and those looking to add the wild cat to their lair of Beanies finally had the chance. But it was short-lived. Blizzard was among the 28 Beanies retired on May 1, 1998. A few lucky fans were able to pick her up later in the summer when she was used in a Chicago White Sox promotion. **RETIRED.**

BONGO THE MONKEY

Ty's little swinger has an interesting tail … uh … tale. Bongo was distributed in two different versions: one with a brownish tail matching his golden brown coat, and another with a lighter tan tail. (An initial release of the tan-tailed monkey was also called Nana; she is extremely rare and valuable.) Needless to say, these changes had collectors going bananas. The monkeys wearing tags from earlier generations are more rare, whether sporting a dark or a light tail. Bongo also appeared in the second collection of McDonald's Teenie Beanies.

CONGO THE GORILLA

Aping around is this Beanie's game. Congo, the black-and-brown gorilla, might first appear to be fierce, but he's really just a big ape in Ty's barrel of monkeys. Displayed alone or with others from the bunch, this primate adds a touch of jungle fever to his posse of more gentle-looking cousins. Can you guess which Beanie Baby he has something in common with? The answer: Bessie the cow. Like Bessie, Congo's birthday is after his release date.

HAPPY THE HIPPO

Fans hungry for this hippo found the stampede was on when Ty announced his retirement in May 1998. Originally gray when Ty released the plush toy, Happy lightened up when he was changed to a lavender color in mid-1995. This fanciful Beanie was also among those released as a Teenie Beanie in the second McDonald's giveaway. **RETIRED.**

FRECKLES THE LEOPARD

This adorable cat is one of the best-loved Beanies. His salmon-colored nose and large, yellow-rimmed black eyes easily stand out among his spots. In a prone position, this native of the jungle appears poised to swat a fly rather than track down prey. A collector's tip: Some of the leopards were shipped with the wrong birthday printed on the tag—July 28, 1996, rather than June 3, 1996.

HUMPHREY THE CAMEL

This tan camel with long, floppy legs looks as though he's just collapsed from the heat; he truly can't stand on his own four feet! Collectors may feel just as leg-weary after they've searched the world's deserts seeking this odd-looking character. This plush dromedary has risen considerably in price after retirement, and he ranks as one of the most difficult items to find in Ty's Beanie line. **RETIRED.**

KIWI THE TOUCAN

This radiant bird is a long way from home. A native of South and Central America, he has become a favorite throughout the Beanie nation. Although highly sought-after, Kiwi isn't a bird of distinction. He travels as the crow flies, sharing the same body style as Caw the crow. What makes this old bird stand out in the menagerie? His colorful beak and tail. Some tags on third-generation Kiwis also have his name spelled completely in lowercase. **RETIRED.**

PEANUT THE ELEPHANT

An elephant may never forget, but when it came to this little Beanie, some-body sure did. Peanut suffered a case of the blues when Ty mistakenly released the plush elephant in a bright royal blue. Redesigned in a lighter shade, the baby-blue pachyderm with pink, flappy ears was one of the May 1, 1998, retirees. Those fortunate to have one of the earlier models can toot their horns—the royal-blue Peanut has skyrocketed in value. The baby-blue Peanut can be found among the second McDonald's Teenie Beanie collection.

RETIRED.

ROARY THE LION

Ty's king of the jungle had collectors roaring when he made his debut on the *Today* show a few weeks before the official announcement of his release. Golden brown with a rich, furry mane (similar to the texture of Nuts the squirrel's tail), Roary's beauty makes it apparent why this cat has been crowned king. If you're look-ing for a leader of your Beanie pack, you can't go wrong with this cat.

SPIKE THE RHINOCEROS

When Spike horned in on the action, Beanie fever was at a high pitch. He swiftly disappeared from the shelves. Big-game hunters in search of this thick-skinned Beanie were snatching him up as soon as he hit the retail market. More frequent sightings of the grayish brown rhino might be a sign that it's time for him to retire for good.

TWIGS THE GIRAFFE

It took only a few Twigs for this Beanie to set the world of collecting ablaze. The bright orange-and-yellow herbivore can often be found standing tall in a pile of current Beanies. But don't expect him to be around for long. Ty retired Twigs in May 1998. And with his release among the second batch of Teenie Beanies, it's certain that this bean-filled baby can only grow in popularity. **RETIRED.**

STRIPES THE TIGER

Ty's tiger pawed his way through the jungle of cats in this kingdom of bean-stuffed animals. Originally issued in a dark orange with thin black stripes, he was later reissued in a lighter peach tone with thick black stripes. Why? It's hard to say. But it's not hard to say which version is more desirable. After his May 1998 retirement, the original dark orange cat will have collectors clawing the corners of the earth to snare him for their zoos. **RETIRED.**

VELVET THE PANTHER

Black as night, this jungle cat, with her peach-colored nose and yellow-ringed black eyes, truly stands out in a display of Beanie Babies. Predators searching out this sleek cat most likely still can find her lurking about, even after her October 1997 retirement. But don't be fooled by her docile manner— Velvet is just as sassy as the other cats in Ty's jungle. **RETIRED.**

ZIGGY THE ZEBRA

This Beanie made headlines when Ty switched his coat to a broader-striped fabric. Ziggy, the black-and-white (what else?) zebra, helped Ty fill its zoo with animals from A–Z. Available until the May 1, 1998, retirement, this Beanie can be found among most collections. If you've yet to add him to yours, do so before he zigs away for good. **RETIRED.**

Down on the Farm

These Beanie Babies aren't ready to be put out to pasture yet. Strut the rooster signals the sunrise to his farmyard friends. Below him, Fleece the lamb keeps an eye on the flock. Tabasco the bull and Daisy the cow rest in the barn while their friend Bessie takes a break on a bale of hay. Next to the barn, Gobbles the turkey and Grunt the razorback play in the dirt as Caw the crow swoops low over the field. Derby the horse and Squealer the pig indulge in a drink at the watering trough while Chops the lamb dreams of greener pastures.

BESSIE THE COW

It's no bull that this little lady is "udderly" divine. The brown-and-white Jersey with pink horns (which were darkened noticeably after her initial release) is part of the Beanie farm-animal collection. The cuddly critter, whose unexpected retirement left many collectors blazing trails to find her, is the second cow in the line. (Daisy, the black cow, was released a year earlier.) However, those hoping to find Bessie grazing among their collections should expect to pay more than her original cost. Notice anything odd about Bessie's birthday? It's after her release date! **RETIRED.**

CAW THE CROW

Was this an ugly duckling...or something to crow about? Caw, a plump, black bird with bright orange beak and webbed feet, is often mistakenly referred to as a black duck, and he is little-known outside Beanie collecting circles. Issued without a poem, this little fellow is a coveted member of the Beanie bunch. Caw lasted only a year before being retired in 1996. **RETIRED.**

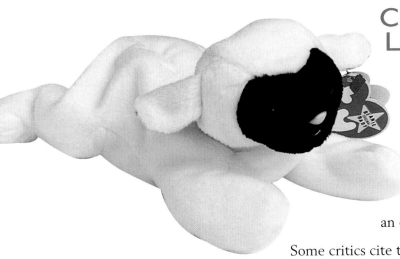

CHOPS THE LAMB

W hat's in a name? This Beanie's moniker might have precipitated an early retirement. Some critics cite too many similarities to Shari Lewis's famous puppet Lamb Chop as the reason behind Ty's "unplanned" retirement of this none-too-sheepish character. Chops was the only Teenie Beanie "mom" to be retired before the first McDonald's Teenie Beanie promotion kicked off. Another tidbit for collectors to sink their teeth into: The word "surely" was misspelled in Chops's poem on some hang tags. **RETIRED.**

DAISY THE COW

H oly cow! Daisy, Ty's black-and-white cow, turned up somewhere other than a farmer's field when the Chicago Cubs gave 10,000 of the bean-stuffed bovines away on May 3, 1998, as a tribute to their late sportscaster Harry Caray. Now, how's that for a moo-ving tribute? The special edition of this spotted lady (she has a white spot on her back) came with a commemorative tag. Other sightings of interest: On very rare occasions a spotless Daisy can be found.

DERBY THE HORSE

Ty horsed around a lot with this Beanie. The company redesigned the light brown horse three times. He first appeared in a very limited production with a mane and tail of soft, thin black yarn. The second release sported a coarser yarn of the same color. The third transformation came about in 1998 when Derby was released with a star (a white spot) on his forehead. With such a varied crop of foals, there's most likely a winner to be found in this herd.

FLEECE THE LAMB

This snow-white, nappy-plushed lamb with a pink nose and mouth replaced Chops when that Beanie met an early retirement. Fleece has also been compared to several celebrated lambs: Remember Mary's little lamb with fleece as white as snow? And then there's the lamb that landed her predecessor in a stew—Shari Lewis's Lamb Chop. Although some collectors think Fleece also favors the famous puppet, the likeness is harder to prove than poor Chops's resemblance.

GOBBLES THE TURKEY

This Thanksgiving offering served as one of Ty's Holiday Beanies in October 1997. With her timely release, the brilliantly colored plush flew off the shelf. Fortunately, it was collectors (and not hungry dinner guests) gobbling up this pretty little bird.

GRUNT THE RAZORBACK

This spiked-back critter had his own cheering section when fans of the University of Arkansas Razorbacks began hogging the four-legged Beanie to use as their sports teams' mascot. Bright red with white felt tusks and black button eyes, this razorback is far less menacing than the one you might find lurking in the brush. Popular with collectors, not just Arkansas fans, this not-so-mean Beanie was retired in May 1997. **RETIRED.**

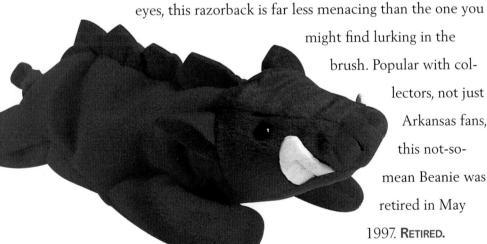

SNORT THE BULL

A red-hot commodity in the Chicago market, collectors are betting on Ty making this one a Chicago Bulls premium. Will they? Only Ty knows for sure. With rumors of more tie-ins to professional sports teams expected, the connection seems likely. Designed in "Bulls" red, this Beanie Baby would be perfectly suited for the job. Collectors stampeded to McDonald's to add this original Teenie Beanie to their herd of plush animals.

SQUEALER THE PIG

This little piggy is a real babe. His light pink plush and darker pink snout and tail had collectors going hog-wild over Squealer. A member of the original nine Beanies, this mud-loving pig really cleaned up when he hit the market. However, with his retirement in May 1998, the little porker will be hard to find before long. The one thing collectors can be certain of: You won't find any footballs being made from this pig's skin. **RETIRED.**

Strut the Rooster

This rooster really knows how to strut his stuff. Originally issued as Doodle, Ty's rooster didn't miss a beat when the bird underwent changes to keep from encroaching upon a fast-food chain's trademark. Designed in tie-dyed colors of coral, hot pink, yellow, magenta, and sometimes green, Strut rose to the occasion, leaving collectors cock-a-doodle-do-ing over the swift transition.

Tabasco the Bull

As hot as the sauce from which he borrowed his name, Tabasco lasted only a year on the shelf. His exit from the Beanie line (due to yet another trademark problem) proved that it was a bullish market for the lucky few who added this one to their collection. The all-red bull was replaced with Snort. How can you tell the two apart? Check out the fancy footwork on Snort—his hooves were changed to white.

Retired.

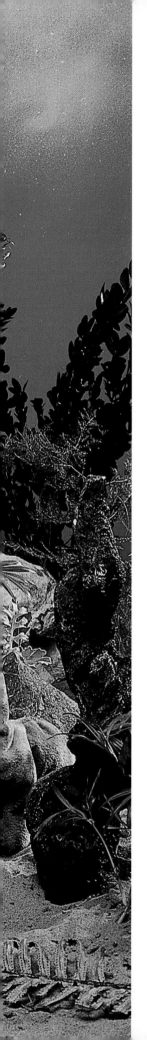

Out of This World

Dinosaurs and mythical creatures inhabit another world—a world of magic and mysticism, fantasy and dreams. This is a world in which ghosts and spirits feel right at home. Mystic the unicorn with iridescent horn (left) and her brown-horned sister perch on a rocky precipice as fine-maned Mystic explores the formations below. Soaring above the scene on iridescent wings, Magic the dragon watches as Steg the stegosaurus, Rex the tyrannosaurus, and Bronty the brontosaurus forage on the sparsely covered ground. Spooky the ghost is lurking at right.

BRONTY THE BRONTOSAURUS

Those seeking the full Bronty will be disappointed. The blue tie-dyed brontosaurus, with gray-and-aqua tinge, was issued without a poem or birthday. However, the smart collector knows that this Beanie (along with his other tie-dyed friends) is truly one of a kind—no two tie-dyed items are ever alike. Hard to find in mint condition, this plush, long-neck herbivore makes for an upstanding addition to any collection. An interesting fact: Bronty shares a style number with Righty the elephant. **RETIRED.**

MAGIC THE DRAGON

You won't see this mythical creature breathing fire. Magic, the white dragon with silvery-pink iridescent wings, is one of the more beautiful Beanies in the collection. Inspired by the dragon made famous in song, Ty's white puff of plush is pure magic. Although the dragon hasn't undergone any major changes, there are a few subtle variations to look for: The pink thread on Magic's nose and wings can be found in pale or hot pink, and earlier versions of the dragon have puffier wings. **RETIRED.**

MYSTIC THE UNICORN

This all-white Beanie horned in on the fun of stumping collectors by appearing in altered states. Ty originally released Mystic with a tan-colored horn and a mane and tail made of fine white yarn. The fine yarn gradually gave way to a coarser grade and, in 1997, the horn was replaced with an iridescent one made of the same material as Magic the dragon's wings.

REX THE TYRANNOSAURUS

This T-Rex is dino-mite! A member of Ty's tie-dyed trio of prehistoric Beanie Babies, Rex is a blast of brilliant colors. His plush coat of various shades of orange, pink, violet, and blue sets him apart from the typical Jurassic crowd. But like that same crowd, you won't find any of these Beanies currently roaming about. Rex was retired almost exactly a year after his release. This dinosaur and Lefty the donkey share the same style number. **RETIRED.**

SPOOKY THE GHOST

This is one friendly ghost! Now all smiles, he once appeared in a variation with his mouth drawn into a ghoulish grimace. It was no trick when Ty gave this little treat a birthday on Halloween! Look for Spooky hanging about with fellow night lovers Spinner the spider and Radar the bat. The trio makes a hauntingly appealing group. The name "Spook" was mistakenly printed on some hang tags. **RETIRED.**

STEG THE STEGOSAURUS

The last in Ty's trio of dinosaurs, Steg was on the market only one year. Yellow, brown, tan, teal, and green, the colorful stegosaurus blends well with his tie-dyed buddies. Although he is retired, the short, plump Beanie is said to still roam some corners of the earth, unlike his extinct mates. Steg sightings in out-of-the-way shops have been reported over the Internet. **RETIRED.**

Marsh Fellows

These "swamp things" are colorful additions to an otherwise waterlogged scene. Scoop the pelican's and Pinky the flamingo's bright orange beaks are "beakons" for their fellow Beanie Babies, drawing them to their meeting place in this tropical marsh. Gracie the swan glides through the water and Smoochy the frog looks on from the safety of a lily pad as Ally the alligator noses his way into the pond. Speedy the turtle and Quackers the duck sun themselves on the near side of the bank, but Hissy the snake is all wrapped up in something else. The little fellow at right is Legs the frog.

ALLY THE ALLIGATOR

This gator has really been around! Ally was released with the second batch of Beanies and retired in October 1997. A favorite among boys, the scaly-backed reptile has certainly experienced his own brand of tough love. It's highly unlikely that you'll find many of these snappy green fellows intact. And although he hasn't undergone any cosmetic changes from the manufacturer, mint-condition Allys with older tags are very difficult to find. **RETIRED.**

GRACIE THE SWAN

Considered too plain by many collectors, Gracie the all-white swan was slow to move off the shelf. However, as part of the May 1, 1998, retirement, Gracie was soon descended upon by flocks of collectors anxious to add this Beanie to their collection. Gracie was also the third Beanie to be used in a Chicago Cubs giveaway; she floated smoothly into Wrigley Field on September 13, 1998. Can you guess which player she honored? Mark my words, it was one with plenty of Grace. **RETIRED.**

HISSY THE SNAKE

This guy is no snake in the grass. Hissy, the spiral-shaped serpent, had kids charmed from the start. They found that wearing him wrapped around their wrists was the perfect way to carry the Beanie. When stretched out of his coiled shape, this Ty baby is the second-longest Beanie in the collection. Fun to play with, this bean-filled plush toy makes for a great pet. How many snakes can you say that about?

LEGS THE FROG

Beanie aficionados who brought this amphibian home to their pads have a leg up on latecomers to the world of Beanie mania. Ty's leaf-green frog was one of the original nine Beanie Babies introduced in 1994. Considered plain in comparison to some of his plush pals, Legs nevertheless hung around the pond for quite a while. He was finally retired in October 1997. **RETIRED.**

SPEEDY THE TURTLE

Interest in this Beanie Baby sped up when he became one of the Teenie Beanies launched in the first McDonald's promotional giveaway. One of the smallest Beanies, Speedy, with his green body and brown-shelled back, crept along at a snail's pace for quite some time, finally retiring in October 1997. Just like in the famous fable, this turtle might surprise collectors down the road and come out the big winner. **RETIRED.**

PINKY THE FLAMINGO

You won't find this flamingo balancing on one leg in your lawn. Pinky, Ty's hot-pink bird with orange beak and long legs, has been hard to come by for many collectors. She was one of the more difficult original Teenie Beanies to find as well. Pretty in pink, this bird will dress up any collection.

SCOOP THE PELICAN

The scoop on this bird is that his popularity has increased since his release as a Teenie Beanie in the second flock of McDonald's giveaways. The awkward-looking, bluish gray bird with the protruding gold bill initially wasn't a very popular Beanie Baby with collectors. However, Ty found a way to make them swallow him up. Don't wait until this one has flown off the current list to try to find him.

SMOOCHY THE FROG

This frog must have been kissed by a princess, because he sure is a prince compared to the plainer-looking Legs. Smoochy is fashioned after the tree frogs native to Costa Rica and South America, and he makes a colorful addition to Ty's pond. Still current, this log-loving amphibian has yet to leap in value. However, don't underestimate the long-distance jumper; he's still highly desirable.

QUACKERS THE DUCK

This bird's wings were literally clipped before he could fly. Ty's bright yellow duck was initially released without wings. When he was reissued with wings, his original version sailed into obscurity, making him highly desirable to collectors. Quackers is one of two Beanies whose Teenie Beanie was released with a different name—Quacks. As if those oddities weren't enough, some Quackers made it off the line without eyes or brows. Was some wisequacker running the assembly line? RETIRED.

The Arctic Circle

This frozen land offers unlimited activities for these snow-loving Beanies. Nanook the husky performs his favorite task as he pulls Snowball the snowman swiftly through the drifts. Puffer the puffin has taken to the sky to watch over her friends Seamore the seal and Waddle the penguin as they skate on thin ice. Tusk the walrus emerges from an igloo to meet Jolly the walrus, who reclines on a snowy bank, while Chilly the polar bear bounds over the freshly fallen snow to join his cold-weather friends.

CHILLY THE POLAR BEAR

It certainly won't be a breeze finding one of these bean-stuffed bears in mint condition. Chilly, an all-white bear, was among the first of the plush toys to launch the wave of Beanie mania. He was also one of the first Beanies to increase substantially in value. Fashioned after the lay down–style bears in the line, few Chillys have survived the grubby little fingers of the children for whom they were originally meant. A mint-condition example of this Arctic bear commands quite a cool price. **RETIRED.**

JOLLY THE WALRUS

Trying to find a Jolly was no laughing matter for those attempting to add Ty's mustachioed walrus to their collection. Retailers just couldn't seem to keep the grayish brown Beanie with bushy lip and white tusks on the shelf. It became obvious that this was one Beanie that could really bring a smile to collectors' faces. But like most good things, Jolly's time eventually came to an end. He was retired on May 1, 1998. **RETIRED.**

NANOOK THE HUSKY

This Alaskan pup caused a blizzard of excitement when he was introduced. Nanook, a white-and-gray husky with blue eyes and pointed ears, had collectors turning to mush over his adorable mug. A member of the popular Beanie Baby dog family, this pup might not be more valuable than any of the other Beanie dogs, but he certainly is one of the favorite pooches in the pack.

PUFFER THE PUFFIN

Ty's puffin is one of the more recent additions to the world of Beanie Babies. Similar to Kiwi the toucan, this black seabird with red-and-yellow beak is ready to find a partner to cuddle with. Like all in her species, she uses her brightly colored beak to signal her single status to potential partners. Take her home and give her a little TLC; she'll love the attention.

SEAMORE THE SEAL

This white sea-pup was another Beanie that didn't surface often. Her snow-white plush ensures that she will be even more difficult to uncover in mint condition as time passes. Collectors won't see many more of this Beanie swimming about; she was retired in October 1997. Land one if you can! **RETIRED.**

SNOWBALL THE SNOWMAN

This little snowball caused quite an avalanche when he was released. Issued with 1997 Holiday Teddy, Spinner the spider, Batty the bat, and Gobbles the turkey, Snowball rounded out Ty's 1997 holiday collection and warmed a heart or two. Donned in festive garb, he sports a black felt hat with a bright red band and a bright red scarf with white fringe. Like Holiday Teddy, this Beanie melted before the new year rang in; Ty retired Snowball on December 31, 1997. **RETIRED.**

Tusk the Walrus

Tusk started out his Beanie life tossing in a "c" of confusion. His name appeared as "Tuck" on his hang tag. The little brown walrus's name was corrected, and he went on to live a happy life in Beaniedom. But what about the Tucks? If you netted one, keep it. You'll wind up "c-ing" a nice return on your investment. **Retired.**

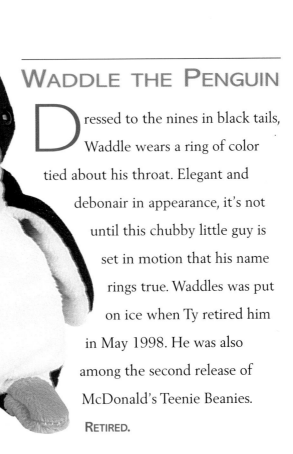

Waddle the Penguin

Dressed to the nines in black tails, Waddle wears a ring of color tied about his throat. Elegant and debonair in appearance, it's not until this chubby little guy is set in motion that his name rings true. Waddles was put on ice when Ty retired him in May 1998. He was also among the second release of McDonald's Teenie Beanies. **Retired.**

The Outback

This collection of Beanie marsupials, desert dwellers, and exotic birds is at home in the sparse foliage of these sandy plains. Rainbow the chameleon blends into his rocky perch, and Lizzy the lizard suns herself on a piece of driftwood as Tank the armadillo and Pouch the kangaroo wander by. Stretch the ostrich stretches her legs on the far side of the river, and Patti the platypus looks ready to go for a swim. Mel the koala has found a comfortable spot in a nearby tree—the same tree Iggy the iguana is attempting to climb!

IGGY THE IGUANA

Switched at birth! It certainly wasn't this iguana's night—or day—when the first shipments of the reptile hit retail. It seems that Iggy, the blue tie-dyed iguana, had switched tags with Rainbow, the multicolored chameleon. Upon further investigation, it appeared that the confusion was caused by their plush pelts: Iggy's body more closely resembled that of a chameleon and Rainbow's that of an iguana. Things were eventually straightened out and the two now live comfortably in their own skins.

LIZZY THE LIZARD

Leaping lizards! This quick-change artist made his debut in muted tie-dye colors of pink, orange, yellow, and green before being re-released in a deep blue with black spots and an orange-and-yellow underbelly. Both lizards have a bright red felt tongue. Lizzy was retired in January 1998. The redesigned lizard was among the first batch of Teenie Beanies issued by McDonald's, but this smaller counterpart was named Lizz. **RETIRED.**

MEL THE KOALA

This tree-dwelling Beanie can be found hiding among the leaves of most savvy Beanie lovers' collections. Although a common sight in the Australian bush, this furry-eared marsupial was difficult to spot when his plush counterpart hit retail. Rumored to be named for the Aussies' most famous Mel (Gibson, that is), this koala is a popular fellow. He was also among the second release of McDonald's Teenie Beanies.

PATTI THE PLATYPUS

Shades of red color this web-footed creature different from most. Patti, one of the original nine Beanie Babies, was a deep fuchsia with a bright gold beak and feet and black button eyes when first released. She soon appeared wearing a shade closer to raspberry, and later sported a darker, magenta color. She was then changed to a lighter fuchsia and can finally rest comfortably in her feathers. Patti was among the May 1, 1998, retirees; she was also one of the original McDonald's Teenie Beanies. **RETIRED.**

POUCH THE KANGAROO

Pouch and her little joey hopped in from the outback to join their Beanie friends. Pouch, Ty's brown-and-white kangaroo, is the only Beanie to come with her own baby. Although rumors of retirement have been constant (there are concerns about the little kangaroo's head coming unsewn from mom's pouch), the pair have remained current. However, one never knows what Ty might do. Those interested in adding this dynamic duo to their collection should hop to it!

RAINBOW THE CHAMELEON

Ty may have been singing over the Rainbow when this colorful fellow was created, but he was somehow tagged Iggy (a case of mistaken identity with Iggy the iguana). Rainbow, the multicolored chameleon, soon discovered that he still didn't have anything to sing about when, after further inspection, it appeared that the two's bodies, and not their tags, were switched. And you thought chameleons only changed colors!

STRETCH THE OSTRICH

This bird makes for a plum(e) addition to any collection. Modeled after Pinky the flamingo, this lanky bird has no need to hide her head in the ground. Stretch, with her long, tanned legs, is sitting pretty among her Beanie companions released in January 1998. Not adhering to the adage "birds of a feather flock together," this oversize bird has certainly taken flight as a desired collectible.

TANK THE ARMADILLO

This Beanie didn't have to get tanked to start seeing double, or triple for that matter. Originally released with seven plates (lines representing ribs), the gray armadillo did a Texas two-step when he was reissued with nine. Still not satisfied, Ty produced a third version with a protective shell and nine plates, and the Tank was finally ready for battle. **Retired.**

Kitty Corner

When their owner's away, these cats will play! Trap the mouse might just regret his entrance into this feline fray—Zip is ready to pounce! Flip dirties his snow-white paws in the leafy plant that shades Pounce, who is relaxing on the rocking chair. Chip the calico cat has found a more comfortable place to curl up, while Nip has gotten up from his catnap to paw at a toy. Snip the Siamese cat unfurls a ball of yarn as Prance gets tangled in his own brand of mischief.

CHIP THE CALICO CAT

A-paws, a-paws for this colorful feline. Ty's calico cat is a splash of black, rust, and white, and she ranks as a member of one of the more popular groups of Beanie Babies. The cat family is the second most popular line of Beanies; any new addition to the litter is considered a "must have" among collectors. An interesting fact for the cat fancier: Chip was among a release that included four dogs.

FLIP THE WHITE CAT

Collectors totally flipped over this ball of white fur. Flip's delicate features (blue eyes and a pink nose, ears, and whiskers) made it hard to resist this feline. When she was retired in October 1997, retailers found it hard to keep this Beanie in stock—and it wasn't her feline curiosity leading her astray! **RETIRED.**

NIP THE GOLD CAT

Catnip must have been on the menu for this dizzy feline. Nip, along with his best friend, Zip, has gone through three design changes. The original gold cat had a fuller head with white muzzle and belly, a pink button nose, mouth, and whiskers, and solid black eyes. The second version was solid gold with a smaller head, pink ears, mouth, and whiskers, and a pink button nose. His eyes were black with a gold outer ring. The last Nip had the same body as the second, but he had white paws, ears, whiskers, and mouth. **RETIRED.**

POUNCE THE CAT

This little kitty pounced into Beaniedom and landed on all fours—at least for now! It seems that the brown tie-dyed cat might be yet another Beanie Baby to run into trademark problems (there's a cat food by the same name). A new name for this cat might be a welcome change for Ty, but fur will be flying as collectors try to add this cat to their litter of Beanies before it's too late.

PRANCE THE CAT

Prance is yet another addition to Ty's feline frenzy. The gray tiger-striped kitten can cause quite a stir; she's easily mistaken for one of the Beanie tigers. But don't let anyone spin any yarns about this little lady. She's definitely a cat, and, with her bright blue eyes and little pink whiskers, she's the purr-fect addition to any Beanie collection.

SNIP THE SIAMESE CAT

That darn cat has nerve! Just like the real thing, Ty's Siamese has plenty of attitude. The champagne-colored cat with blue-ringed black eyes and chocolate-colored points is a beautiful specimen of the Far Eastern breed. And she knows it! Stretched out on all fours, this finicky feline is the only purebred in Ty's cathouse. This pretty kitty is definitely the cat's meow.

TRAP THE MOUSE

If you have this Beanie mouse in your house, you're one of the lucky few. Trap, Ty's little gray-and-pink mouse with whiskers and black eyes, is worth more than his weight in cheese—or gold. This little mouse is the tiniest creature in Ty's field of Beanies. Trap is difficult to find and highly desirable; collectors wanting to add this mighty mouse to their collection should plan on springing big cash to trap him. RETIRED.

ZIP THE BLACK CAT

Ty pawed around with three different versions of this black cat. Zip the black cat with white face and ears was the first in the litter; Zip the solid-black cat with pink ears followed. Last, but not least, Zip was released with his original white ears and some fancy white footwear to match! Zip was retired in May 1998, but he was also a member of the second collection of McDonald's Teenie Beanies released that same month. RETIRED.

Beanie Patriots

These flag-bearing Beanie Babies pay tribute to Canada, America, and England. The trio of bears (left to right), Maple, Libearty, and Britannia, perch proudly on the American flag as the Canadian and British flags provide a patriotic background. Lefty the donkey and Righty the elephant feel right at home among the stars and stripes: These political pundits pay tribute to the Democratic and Republican parties, respectively.

BRITANNIA THE BEAR

God save this Beanie. That is, if you're lucky enough to get your hands on one. This rare bear can be found only in shops in the United Kingdom. As part of the growing "patriotic" clan of Beanies, the new-faced brown bear with the Union Jack flag embroidered on her chest is highly desirable. She's also a dead ringer for Teddy. Shoppers looking to add Britannia to their collection might find that some of the bears have been produced without the Union Jack flag; the only way to differentiate them from Teddy is by their tags.

LIBEARTY THE BEAR

It was a game of words for this particular Beanie. Although released in honor of the Summer Olympic games held in Atlanta in 1996, Libearty was unable to bear the word "Olympic" on her tag when Ty could not obtain permission from the International Olympic Committee. Patriotic to the end, this white bear with American flag emblazoned across her chest and red-and-blue ribbon tied about her neck turned out to be a winner just the same. Worth noting: Libearty was the first Beanie to come with a poem. **RETIRED.**

LEFTY THE DONKEY

It was party time when Ty introduced patriotic Lefty and his counterpart, Righty the elephant. Lefty, the periwinkle donkey with black hooves, nose, ears, mane, and tail, has an American-flag patch on his back. He was released to commemorate the 1996 presidential election along with Righty. However, like some politicians, these Beanies found their careers to be short-lived. Ty retired the two editions six months after they were introduced. RETIRED.

MAPLE THE BEAR

This white bear, originally released with the name "Pride," is quite a patriot. Similar in design to his American counterpart, Libearty, Maple was created to commemorate Canadian Independence Day. Issued only in Canada, the bear, with maple-leaf flag on his chest and red ribbon tied about his neck, was hard for collectors to come by. A limited edition of the bears was also distributed during the last week of August 1997 to help benefit the Special Olympics.

RIGHTY THE ELEPHANT

Elephants really can fly! Righty certainly did when he was introduced with Lefty the donkey to commemorate the 1996 presidential election. It's obvious where this Beanie, dressed in conservative gray, gets his name. Just as his democratic counterpart shares a style number with Rex the tyrannosaurus, Righty shares a style number with Ty's dinosaur Bronty. And check out Righty's flag—it has been spotted flying upside down. RETIRED.

1998 Spring Arrivals

ANTS
THE ANTEATER

EARLY
THE ROBIN

FETCH THE GOLDEN
RETRIEVER

FORTUNE THE PANDA

GIGI
THE POODLE

GLORY
THE BEAR

JABBER
THE PARROT

JAKE
THE MALLARD DUCK

TRACKER
THE BASSET HOUND

KUKU
THE COCKATOO

WHISPER
THE DEER

ROCKET
THE BLUE JAY

WISE
THE OWL

STINGER
THE SCORPION

Teenie Beanies

O n April 11, 1997, McDonald's started a new Happy Meal promotion. With each Happy Meal purchased, customers were rewarded with a smaller version of one of ten Beanie Babies. This set of Teenie Beanies included Teenie Chocolate, Chops, Goldie, Lizz, Patti, Pinky, Quacks, Seamore, Snort, and Speedy.

First set

Planned as a five-week promotion with two Teenie Beanies to be featured each week, McDonald's was forced to call a halt to the giveaway after only ten days because all five weeks' worth of Teenies were gone. Some stores sold out completely in the first weekend! This incredible rush occurred despite the fact that McDonald's, realizing they had underestimated demand, did very little advertising for the promotion.

With this in mind, McDonald's announced a second Happy Meal Teenie Beanie promotion slated to begin May 22, 1998. This set featured Teenie Bones, Bongo, Doby, Happy, Inch, Mel, Peanut, Pinchers, Scoop, Twigs, Waddle, and Zip. In preparation, McDonald's ordered twice the production of each Teenie Beanie— but to no avail. Once again, the Teenies sold out in most McDonald's stores by the end of the first week-end. Rumors have already begun of a third Teenie Beanie promotion in 1999, but one has to wonder just how many Teenies will have to be made in order to keep up with the incredible demand.

Second set

Price List

Ally the alligator	$35–$45		Derby the horse with fine mane	$2,750–$3,250
Ants the anteater	$5–$7		Derby the horse with coarse mane	$20–$25
Baldy the eagle	$12–$15		Derby the horse with a star	$5–$7
Batty the bat	$5–$7		Digger the orange crab	$750–$850
Bernie the St. Bernard	$5–$7		Digger the red crab	$100–$125
Bessie the cow	$50–$60		Doby the doberman	$5–$7
Blackie the bear	$5–$7		Doodle the rooster	$40–$50
Blizzard the tiger	$12–$15		Dotty the Dalmatian	$5–$7
Bones the dog	$12–$15		Early the robin	$5–$7
Bongo the brown-tailed monkey	$50–$60		Ears the brown rabbit	$12–$15
Bongo the tan-tailed monkey	$5–$7		Echo the dolphin	$12–$15
Britannia the bear	$10–$20		Erin the bear	$5–$7
Bronty the brontosaurus	$850–$1,000		Fetch the golden retriever	$5–$7
Brownie the bear	$3,750–$4,000		Flash the dolphin	$100–$125
Bruno the dog	$5–$7		Fleece the lamb	$5–$7
Bubbles the fish	$120–$150		Flip the white cat	$30–$40
Bucky the beaver	$30–$40		Floppity the lilac bunny	$12–$15
Bumble the bee	$550–$650		Flutter the butterfly	$900–$1,100
Caw the crow	$600–$700		Fortune the panda	$5–$7
Chilly the polar bear	$1,750–$2,000		Freckles the leopard	$5–$7
Chip the calico cat	$5–$7		Garcia the bear	$175–$200
Chocolate the moose	$5–$7		Gigi the poodle	$5–$7
Chops the lamb	$140–$180		Glory the bear	$5–$7
Claude the crab	$5–$7		Gobbles the turkey	$5–$7
Congo the gorilla	$5–$7		Goldie the goldfish	$35–$45
Coral the fish	$150–$180		Gracie the swan	$12–$15
Crunch the shark	$5–$7		Grunt the razorback	$150–$175
Cubbie the bear	$22–$30		Happy the gray hippo	$750–$850
Curly the bear	$5–$7		Happy the lavender hippo	$15–$20
Daisy the cow	$5–$7			

Hippity the mint bunny	$12–$15
Hissy the snake	$5–$7
Hoot the owl	$40–$50
Hoppity the rose bunny	$12–$15
Humphrey the camel	$1,800–$2,000
Iggy the iguana	$5–$7
Inch the inchworm with felt antennae	$175–$200
Inch the inchworm with yarn antennae	$12–$15
Inky the tan octopus without a mouth	$800–$950
Inky the tan octopus with a mouth	$650–$750
Inky the pink octopus	$25–$35
Jabber the parrot	$5–$7
Jake the mallard duck	$5–$7
Jolly the walrus	$12–$15
Kiwi the toucan	$160–$190
Kuku the cockatoo	$5–$7
Lefty the donkey	$250–$300
Legs the frog	$20–$25
Libearty the bear	$325–$375
Lizzy the tie-dyed lizard	$900–$1,100
Lizzy the blue lizard	$20–$25
Lucky the ladybug with 7 felt spots	$200–$225
Lucky the ladybug with 21 printed spots	$550–$650
Lucky the ladybug with 11 printed spots	$20–$25
Magic the dragon	$40–$50
Manny the manatee	$150–$175
Maple the bear	$7–$15
Mel the koala	$5–$7
Mystic the unicorn with fine mane	$225–$275
Mystic the unicorn with brown horn	$30–$40
Mystic the unicorn with iridescent horn	$5–$7

Nana the tan-tailed monkey	$3,500–$4,000
Nanook the husky	$5–$7
1997 Holiday Teddy	$35–$45
Nip the gold cat with white face	$500–$600
Nip the gold cat	$850–$950
Nip the gold cat with white paws	$20–$25
Nuts the squirrel	$5–$7
Patti the maroon platypus	$700–$1,000
Patti the fuchsia platypus	$15–$20
Peace the bear	$5–$7
Peanut the royal blue elephant	$4,500–$5,000
Peanut the light blue elephant	$12–$15
Peking the panda	$1,750–$2,250
Pinchers the lobster	$15–$20
Pinky the flamingo	$5–$7
Pouch the kangaroo	$5–$7
Pounce the cat	$5–$7
Prance the cat	$5–$7
Princess the bear	$5–$7
Puffer the puffin	$5–$7
Pugsly the pug dog	$5–$7
Punchers the lobster	$4,000–$4,750
Quackers the wingless duck	$1,750–$2,250
Quackers the duck with wings	$12–$15
Radar the bat	$150–$175
Rainbow the chameleon	$5–$7
Rex the tyrannosaurus	$850–$1,000
Righty the elephant	$250–$300
Ringo the raccoon	$5–$7
Roary the lion	$5–$7
Rocket the blue jay	$5–$7
Rover the dog	$12–$15
Scoop the pelican	$5–$7
Scottie the Scottish terrier	$25–$30
Seamore the seal	$125–$150

Seaweed the otter	$5–$7
Slither the snake	$1,900–$2,100
Sly the brown-bellied fox	$175–$200
Sly the white-bellied fox	$5–$7
Smoochy the frog	$5–$7
Snip the Siamese cat	$5–$7
Snort the bull	$5–$7
Snowball the snowman	$25–$35
Sparky the Dalmatian	$125–$150
Speedy the turtle	$25–$35
Spike the rhinoceros	$5–$7
Spinner the spider	$5–$7
Splash the whale	$100–$125
Spooky the ghost	$30–$35
Spot the dog without a spot	$1,900–$2,100
Spot the dog with a spot	$50–$60
Spunky the cocker spaniel	$5–$7
Squealer the pig	$25–$30
Steg the stegosaurus	$750–$900
Sting the stingray	$160–$190
Stinger the scorpion	$5–$7
Stinky the skunk	$5–$7
Stretch the ostrich	$5–$7
Stripes the tiger with thin stripes (dark)	$275–$325
Stripes the tiger with wide stripes (light)	$12–$15
Strut the rooster	$5–$7
Tabasco the bull	$175–$225
Tank the armadillo with 7 lines and no shell	$175–$200
Tank the armadillo with 9 lines and no shell	$175–$225
Tank the armadillo with shell	$65–$80

Teddy the old-faced brown bear	$2,900–$3,250
Teddy the new-faced brown bear	$75–$100
Teddy the old-faced cranberry bear	$1,750–$2,000
Teddy the new-faced cranberry bear	$1,850–$2,200
Teddy the old-faced jade bear	$1,750–$2,000
Teddy the new-faced jade bear	$1,850–$2,200
Teddy the old-faced magenta bear	$1,750–$2,000
Teddy the new-faced magenta bear	$1,850–$2,200
Teddy the old-faced teal bear	$1,750–$2,000
Teddy the new-faced teal bear	$1,850–$2,200
Teddy the old-faced violet bear	$1,750–$2,000
Teddy the new-faced violet bear	$1,850–$2,200
Tracker the basset hound	$5–$7
Trap the mouse	$1,300–$1,500
Tuffy the terrier	$5–$7
Tusk the walrus	$140–$175
Twigs the giraffe	$12–$15
Valentino the bear	$5–$7
Velvet the panther	$25–$35
Waddle the penguin	$12–$15
Waves the whale	$12–$15
Web the spider	$1,400–$1,700
Weenie the dachshund	$20–$30
Whisper the deer	$5–$7
Wise the owl	$5–$7
Wrinkles the bulldog	$5–$7
Ziggy the zebra	$15–$25
Zip the black cat with white face	$550–$650
Zip the black cat	$1,750–$2,100
Zip the black cat with white paws	$30–$45